FROM RELIGION

TO CHRIST

FROM RELIGION
TO CHRIST

PETER JEFFERY

CALVARY PRESS
Amityville, New York

First printing in August 1994

CALVARY PRESS
P.O. Box 805
Amityville, NY 11701
1-800-789-8175

ISBN 1-879737-13-2

2 4 6 8 10 9 7 5 3 1

Cover and book design by Michael Rotolo

Publisher's special thanks to:

Ron Septimus and Lizanne Webb of Digital Image of
Long Island City, New York for their kind donation of
time and services and their keen personal interest in seeing
the cover art to this book printed with excellence.

PRINTED AND BOUND IN THE UNITED STATES OF AMERICA

CONTENTS

An Introductory Word

This book has now come into your hands. In what condition does it find you? By that question I am asking for your condition in the eyes of God, not of your friends or family, or even yourself.

This book was written by a pastor in Wales who wants to help people come to a true, saving experience of Jesus Christ. He is deeply concerned that the world is filled with multitudes of people who are religious but not redeemed. He has written very simply so that you will understand. But in order to help you, I want to offer you the following suggestions:

First, before you begin reading this book, open your Bible and read John 2:23 - 3:21. Keep this portion of your Bible open whenever you pick up this book to read. The Bible is the sole authority for faith (what we believe) and life (how we live). It was written by men chosen by God to communicate His will perfectly.

Second, I urge you to pray for light from the Lord whenever you pick up this book to read. Prayer is the key given by God to open the treasures contained in the Word. Pray with the words of the psalmist: *"Open my eyes that I may see wonderful things from Your law"* (Ps. 119:18). Read as well Proverbs 2:1-6 and make note of the requirements for attaining the wisdom and knowledge of God.

Third, I invite you to be prepared to lay this book aside at times when you are aware of the Lord speaking directly to *your* conscience. Use this little book as an instrument to bring you close to the Lord.

Finally, I recommend that you seek out a church where God's Word is held as the sole standard for truth and righteousness. God's true people will always be found gathered in humility before His Holy Word.

May you come to know the power of the Gospel within your own heart and life as you seek the Lord diligently with all your being!

The Publishers

NICODEMUS:
THE PHARISEE

John chapter three is probably one of the most well known chapters in the Bible. Most Christians could give an accurate account of the conversation between Jesus and Nicodemus, and most could repeat the sixteenth verse from memory. Here we find Jesus and the Pharisee having an earnest and serious conversation, and Jesus proceeding to teach this man what is one of the most basic doctrines of the Christian faith - the doctrine of regeneration, of being born again.

A man can be ignorant of many things in the Bible and still be saved but J. C. Ryle says "To be ignorant of the matters handled in this chapter, is to be on the broad way which leads to destruction."[1] We do not become Christians as a result of Bible knowledge or of understanding theology but Jesus says if we are to be Christians we *must* be born again. There is no such thing as born again Christians and non-born again Christians. We cannot become

Christians without this new birth. When Jesus said, *must*, he meant there was no alternative. This is why this chapter is so important.

Basically the chapter tells us of one man alone with Jesus. Here is one individual in the presence of the Savior. The next chapter speaks of a woman who had a similar experience. The man and the woman were intellectually, morally and socially, poles apart, but what they had in common, namely an encounter with Jesus, was of far more importance and of lasting consequence than anything else that was true of them. The whole purpose of the Christian Gospel is to bring men and women to Jesus. We all need a personal encounter with the Savior and the message of the Gospel is that it is just as possible for us as it was for Nicodemus.

The Pharisee

The first verse gives us the formal details of this man. Nicodemus was a Pharisee, a member of the Jewish ruling council. He was a religious leader and teacher. This is made clear in verse ten. He is a man of prominence in the community. The Pharisees were a very strict religious group who bitterly opposed Jesus. Almost every reference to them in New Testament finds them contradicting Him. It was this group who, along with the priests, took a prominent part in planning His death. They were very religious but Jesus called them hypocrites. He said they were white washed sepulchers (a stone casket): all nice and clean on the outside but inside full of dead men's bones.

Nicodemus: The Pharisee

The Pharisees were very much a salvation by works party. They could not understand Christ's message of grace, of the free unmerited gift of God, for they had reduced the glorious God-given religion of the Jews to a set of man-made laws, many of which were quite ridiculous. The Bible commentator William Hendriksen tells us this was especially true about their Sabbath laws. For example a woman was not permitted to look in a mirror on the Sabbath because she might see a gray hair and be tempted to pull it out, which would be considered working, and an egg laid on the Sabbath could only be eaten if you killed the hen.

Nicodemus belonged to this religious group. So what was he doing coming to Jesus? Was he beginning to see the emptiness of his religion. It is clear in v. 2 that he had heard and seen something of the ministry of Jesus. Was he now beginning to see how pathetic the man-made religion of the Pharisees was compared to this man's teaching?

Man is a strange and ingenious creature who has created many wonderful things in this world, but has also created many evil things. Of all man's creations nothing is so vile and evil as man-made religion. Whether it be Phariseeism, Hinduism, Islam or the many distortions of Christianity, the result of man-made religion is always to reduce God to our size, to make God manageable. And it is always a salvation by works religion. Consequently it takes men away from God. It leaves men and women with no Savior and no answer to their sin and guilt.

The nonsense of Phariseeism is clear to see, but do we see how equally ridiculous is much of man-distorted Christianity? For instance, does the sprinkling of a few drops of

11

water on a baby's head really make it a Christian? Does going to church now and again, or even every week make a sinner right with God? Isn't that as ridiculous as the Pharisees' gray hair and the egg? Is it not reducing the glorious faith of Jesus to an empty formalism? Is this all we understand by Biblical Christianity? Is it merely enough to call ourselves Methodists or Baptists, Catholics or Anglicans, or even Evangelicals? Is that all God requires of us? Or are you beginning to see the emptiness of *all* man-made religion? Are you questioning your so-called faith and asking "Is this all there is?" Are you beginning to long for a real experience of God, something more than religion is giving you? What does your religion do for you in the stress of work during the week? How does your religion cope with suffering and death? Does it have an answer that really satisfies you and leaves you with peace and hope?

No Hope

Man-made religion will always leave a person where it left Nicodemus. According to Jesus in verse 3 it left Nicodemus with no hope of seeing heaven and therefore on the way to hell. If he continued as he was, good, respectable, religious, moral, he would never see heaven. Think of that for this man whose whole life was steeped in religion! Why did Jesus say this? Because man-made religion has no answer to man's greatest problem which is sin. Man's greatest problem is that because of his sin he is unacceptable to the Holy God. And Jesus in this chapter says that the consequence of our sin is that we perish (v. 16) and are already under the just condemnation of God (v. 18). Man-made religion will always leave us in this world without God and without hope (Eph. 2:12).

Confusion

It will also leave us in a state of total confusion and bewilderment as to spiritual truths. When Jesus speaks to Nicodemus of man's most basic and fundamental need in his relationship to God, the need for a new birth, the need to be born again, Nicodemus is totally confused (see v. 4). He cannot understand spiritual concepts and he interprets them in a literal way that makes them appear nonsense. This is a religious teacher and Jesus has exploded a theological bomb in his mind - "you must be born again." This bombshell shatters Nicodemus and he totters in utter confusion and misunderstanding (v. 4).

It is still the same when religious people are confronted with basic Biblical doctrines on how to become a Christian. When a person hears the true Gospel, who has been taught all his life that Christianity is simply a matter of doing your best, caring for the poor and starving, and going to church now and again, it is so revolutionary, so new, so strange that it explodes in his mind causing a cross between bewilderment and panic. All sorts of counter questions flood into his mind which are as irrelevant and absurd as Nicodemus', "surely he cannot enter a second time into his mother's womb to be born." What Nicodemus is doing is not thinking but reacting in such a way as to shut out the truth of the Gospel. Many still do the same thing. To them Jesus says, as he did to Nicodemus, THINK! Christianity never by-passes a man's mind. It demands that we think, that we apply our minds as well as our hearts to God's truth. Here he goes on to explain exactly what it means to be born again and why it is so essential.

Emptiness

Here then is a man with plenty of formal religion but with no real experience of God. So what brings him to Jesus? Perhaps it was an awareness of the emptiness of his life. His religion was not filling this emptiness. It could not. No more than drink or drugs or a hectic round of social activities can fill and satisfy. The empty life is empty because it lacks God. Nicodemus had his fill of religion and probably he had many friends, enough money and plenty of things to do and places to go but still his life was empty. Then in his emptiness he comes into contact with Jesus. Not the personal contact we see in this chapter but the first contact alluded to in verse 2, and which points back to 2:23-25.[2] He first hears of Jesus, then he observes Him, and he is impressed. Nicodemus is going through life quite happily with his religion. He does not know anything better. What he has is clearly superior to the religion he sees in foreigners but really he is living in the confines of his man-made religion. But then he hears of Jesus. He cannot understand everything about Jesus but two things stand out and he mentions them in v. 2. The teaching and the power of Jesus are so extraordinary that there is only one possible explanation - God is with Him. So he has a very high estimation of Jesus.

What do *you* think of Jesus?

Do you regard Him as a great man, an exceptional man? Do you have a lofty and high view of Jesus?

Jesus once asked His apostles in Matt. 16, whom do men say that I am? That is to ask- What is the current, popular opinion of Me? The answer was somewhat encouraging. Some people said Jesus was John the Baptist come back from the dead. Others said He was Elijah or Jeremiah. All these were great and exceptional men but of course these opinions were wrong and all pitiably inadequate. It is possible to have a very high estimation of Jesus and still be wrong. Who is Jesus? He is God. He is Emmanuel, God with us. So then His teaching is the Word of the living God and when Jesus says you *MUST* be born again, you *MUST*. **Are you?**

Our response to the teaching of Jesus will always be conditioned by whether or not we believe Jesus is the Son of God. This is made very clear in John chapter six. Here were people with a very high opinion of Jesus and they were prepared to take up arms and make him king (vv. 14,15). Yet when he begins to teach them basic Christian doctrine their reaction in v. 60 is "this is a hard teaching. Who can accept it?", and they leave Jesus and no longer follow him (v. 66). The reason for this is that though they were greatly impressed with Jesus they saw him as no more than a man (see v. 42). Compare this estimation with that

15

of a true believer in v. 69 "We believe and know that you are the Holy One of God."

If you believe that, then you must take Him seriously when He says that in order to be Christians, *we must be born again.*

BORN AGAIN

Up until the nineteen sixties the phrase "born again" would only have been heard in an evangelical church or on the lips of Bible believing Christians. But in recent years it has had a far more popular airing. It has been hijacked by the media and largely become a term of ridicule and scorn. There are several reasons for this.

Probably the beginning of this popular airing was its use in American politics. The "born again vote" as it is called in the USA suddenly became very significant and politicians, to win this vote, courted born again Christians. Many politicians claimed to be born again and their "testimonies" were printed in Christian magazines. The moral and political behavior of some of these "born again" men brought being born again into disrepute. Evangelicals in Britain have not helped. They became very quick to parade pop stars and sports stars as born again Christians if they showed the slightest interest in religion. Some may be truly born again but the lives of many have also served to bring being born again into disrepute. So the maligning of the phrase is partly the fault of evangelical Christians themselves.

Different Steps

Also it does not help if Christians do not understand exactly what it means to be born again. Many simply equate it with being converted or being saved, and the terms become interchangeable as if they all mean exactly the same thing. They do *not* mean the same. Born again is not the same as conversion, no more than justification is exactly the same as redemption. The distinguished New Testament scholar, John Murray, reminds us that "when we think of the application of redemption we must not think of it as one simple and indivisible act. It comprises a series of acts and processes. To mention some, we have calling, regeneration, justification, adoption, sanctification, glorification. These are all distinct, and not one of these can be defined in terms of the other. Each has its own distinct meaning, function and purpose in the action and grace of God."[3]

These different and distinct steps must start somewhere, and to quote Prof. Murray again, "regeneration is the beginning of all saving grace *in us*, and all saving grace in exercise on our part proceeds from the fountain of regeneration. We are not born again by faith or repentance or conversion: we repent and believe because we have been regenerated."[4] Faith, repentance, belief are all things that

God demands we do. They are our response to the Gospel. But we cannot do them if we are dead in sin. In order to be able to respond to spiritual truths we must first be born again. This precedes everything and it is the work of God alone. It has to be. The word translated "again", literally means "from above". New birth is the work of God the Holy Spirit. So then being born again is the initial step in salvation. Jesus is telling us that man in sin does not need patching up with religion, morality or education. He needs a complete new beginning. Man had a beginning once in Adam. That was good but it was ruined by sin. We need to be born again, with an ability again to respond to God. This is exactly what the Gospel offers us, and only the Gospel can do this. Sometimes you hear of a man making a new start in life. He changes his home and his job and says he is making a new start. But he is not. He is changing many things but he cannot change his nature. Spiritual new birth gives the sinner a new start with a new nature, a new heart. This can only be done by God.

Spiritual Birth

The new birth is a spiritual birth, it is not a physical birth as Nicodemus seems to think in v. 4. Yet it is interesting to parallel the two types of birth, for the physical sheds light on the spiritual. For instance, in our physical birth we contribute nothing. It was the result of a process initiated by our parents. So too in the spiritual birth. It is initiated by God our heavenly Father. We are born *from above.* This is made clear in John 1:12&13, "yet to all who received him, to those who believed in his name, he gave the right to become children of God - children born not of natural descent, nor of human decision or a husband's will, but born of God."

Without a physical birth we could have no physical existence; so too without a spiritual birth we have no spiritual life. Man is born in sin with a nature already alien to God. We are spiritually dead. New birth gives us a spiritual existence.

You Must Be Born Again

The statement of Jesus is so important that it is worth our while to look at it word by word.

Take the first word YOU and bear in mind who it is Jesus is addressing. Very often religious people will say, we can see that criminals and drug addicts and people like that need a new beginning because of the mess they have made of their lives. But we are not like that. We are honest, industrious, respectable, therefore we do not need to be born again.

This is a very common response to the question of being born again. But Jesus is speaking to Nicodemus a religious leader of the Jews, a man admired and respected and probably quite rightly so. This man needed to be born again, as much as any drug addict or criminal, and so do we all.

There are no exceptions to this. Without this spiritual birth there is no spiritual life. There can be religious life and moral life but there will be no spiritual life.

Consider now the word MUST. Why must? Why is
Jesus so insistent upon this. He does not bring new birth
before Nicodemus, as an option for him to consider. The
eternal Son of God said to this religious man, and says to
everyone, you *MUST* be born again. The reason for this
imperative is given in v. 6, "Flesh gives birth to flesh, but
the Spirit gives birth to spirit." Jesus is saying that sinful
human nature can only produce sinful human nature. J.C.
Ryle wrote that, "Human nature is so utterly fallen, corrupt, and carnal, that nothing can come from it by natural
generation, but a fallen, corrupt, and carnal offspring. There
is no self-curative power in man. He will always go on
reproducing himself. To become spiritual and fit for communion with God, nothing less is required than the entrance
of the spirit of God into our hearts. In one word, we must
have the new birth of the spirit which our Lord twice described to Nicodemus."

The truth of this ought to be obvious to us all. Man is a
sinner and left to himself will always remain a sinner. He
cannot change himself nor his offspring. Flesh is flesh.
Educate it, cultivate it, put it in better surroundings but it
will always remain human nature. It may be physically
beautiful flesh or moral flesh but it is still flesh. That which
is born of the flesh is flesh.

The consequence of this is devastating. Paul argues in
Romans 8:8 "those controlled by the sinful nature (flesh)
cannot please God." This is why we *MUST* be born again,
because left in our sinful human nature we *cannot* please
God. Some people may object 'does this mean that unless
I am born again nothing I can do can please God. If I give

$1,000 to some charity will that not please God?' The answer of the Bible is very clear. Neither the gift nor anything else will please God in the sense that it makes you, a sinner, acceptable to the Holy God. People have great difficulty understanding this because they seek to interpret spiritual truths with an unspiritual mind. Jesus tells Nicodemus that this was his problem. You are a teacher but you cannot understand these things. Nicodemus was interpreting a spiritual truth in a physical way and the result was confusion and bewilderment. He could not understand or appreciate the things of God, and this is true of all who are not born again. Listen to Romans 8:5-7, "Those who live according to the sinful nature have their minds set on what that nature desires; but those who live in accordance with the Spirit have their minds set on what the Spirit desires. The mind of sinful man is death, but the mind controlled by the Spirit is life and peace, because the sinful mind is hostile to God. It does not submit to God's law, nor can it do so." Or consider 1 Corinthians 2:14, "The man without the Spirit does not accept the things that come from the Spirit of God, for they are foolishness to him and he cannot understand them, because they are spiritually discerned".

It is very easy to test these things in our own experiences. Why do people object to being called sinners? Why do people think there is no need to be born again? Why are people outraged to be told they cannot please God?

It is because our thinking is not in line with the thinking of God. We cannot understand these things and we never will unless we are born again. This is why the new

birth is a *MUST*. Left in this spiritual darkness and confusion we will never be able to enter the kingdom of God (v.
5). We will be forever outside God's kingdom and that
means forever in hell. This again underlines the necessity
of being born again. There is no alternative to the new birth.

Effects of the New Birth

What does being born again do to change this awful
condition? First of all it brings spiritual life where previously there was spiritual death. Man because of sin is dead
to God. Listen to the strength of Paul's words in Ephesians
2:1-3. He is reminding these Christians of what they were
like before they were born again, "As for you, you were
dead in your transgressions and sins, in which you used to
live when you followed the ways of this world and of the
ruler of the kingdom of the air, the spirit who is now at
work in those who are disobedient. All of us also lived
among them at one time, gratifying the cravings of our sinful nature and following its desires and thoughts. Like the
rest, we were by our nature objects of God's wrath."

This explains why natural man cannot understand the
things of God. Other standards, other influences dominate
our thinking; influences which feed and encourage our sinful nature and keep us in spiritual darkness, and keep us
spiritually dead. There is only one cure for death and it is
not religion, nor education, nor culture. The only answer
is *life*. Man can supply plenty of religion, education and
culture but life comes only from God. If you take Ephesians

2:1-3 seriously it will lead you to the conclusion that this is an impossible situation to be in. That is perfectly true. Left to man it is impossible. Thank God for the 'but' of v. 4. God alone can change things and He does it by giving the sinner a new birth. He makes us alive in Christ (v. 5), and this new birth takes away the blinders of sin so that we begin to understand spiritual truths (Romans 8:5).

New birth also enables us, now that we are no longer spiritually dead, to respond to the spiritual truths that we are beginning to understand. We can believe now and have faith in Christ. A man who is spiritually dead may admire or like the Gospel but God does not call upon us to admire the Gospel. He commands us to believe it and repent.

How Do We Become Born Again?

To answer this let us consider 1 Peter 1:23-25, "For you have been born again, not of perishable seed, but of imperishable, through the living and enduring word of God. For, 'All men are like grass, and all their glory is like the flowers of the field; the grass withers and the flowers fall, but the word of the Lord stands for ever.' Peter also parallels physical and spiritual birth. How does physical birth come about? By the planting of man's seed in a woman. Peter calls this perishable seed. It will not last forever. Spiritual birth also needs a seed to be planted. This seed is the imperishable word of God, which (v. 25) lasts forever. The implanting comes via the preaching of the Word.

Born Again

This is how God works new birth. He brings sinners under the sound of the Word. "Faith comes through hearing the message" (Romans 10:17). The Gospel shows us our true condition. All have sinned, the good respectable people and the moral outcasts. The Word convinces us that we need to be born again. Only in the Word of God are we shown what God has done in and through the Lord Jesus Christ to deal with our sin.

So if a man wants to be born again, he must go to the Word of God. He must read it, hear it preached and obey it. The Word will turn the seeker of new life of God, to Jesus the only Savior.

THE EVIDENCE OF NEW BIRTH

How do we know if someone is born again? What are the signs that lead one to believe that this great work of God has taken place? This question needs to be addressed for three very important reasons.

First of all, for the sake of the Christian who lacks assurance or for some reason loses assurance. This is not an uncommon problem. After doubts and uncertainty he asks, am I really a Christian? Have I been born again?

Secondly, for the benefit of those who think they are Christians but are not. Many base their Christianity on sandy soil. They never take seriously the question of their sin and guilt and pay little attention to this statement of Jesus that you must be born again in order to be a Christian. Their delusion needs to be challenged and they need to be shown from the scriptures the signs of true faith.

Thirdly, so that when a profession of faith is made Christians may have some guidelines to indicate whether or not it is a genuine work of God.

I want to answer the question in two ways. Firstly to examine the First Epistle of John to see the evidences of new birth as John very clearly spells them out. Secondly to once again parallel physical birth with spiritual birth.

John's First Epistle

A person makes a profession of faith and claims that he is now born again. He has become a Christian. It is always good to hear such claims but an experienced Christian will know that you cannot take this on its face value. It is not being cynical but being realistic and being responsible. You have to look for evidence that this profession is genuine. I do not mean to say that the person is necessarily trying to deceive. *He* may be very genuine and sincere and yet his profession be mistaken. By genuine, I mean that it is not merely the result of emotionalism. Some people get very emotionally moved in a service, particularly in a large evangelistic campaign, and they make a profession of faith. If it is simply the result of the emotion then it will not last. No one can have a saving encounter with Jesus without the emotions being involved but that is not the same thing as emotionalism when only the emotions are involved. Such a profession will soon prove to be false.

By genuine I mean that it is not the product of pressure put on the person by well meaning but irresponsible Christians. Such pressure nearly always by-passes the mind, ignores the biblical demand for repentance and is only concerned with obtaining a decision for Christ.

By genuine I mean that this is a true work of the Holy Spirit, because being born again means being born from above. When someone makes a profession of faith you have to look for signs of spiritual life. By saying he is born again a person is making a most profound claim. He is saying: I was once spiritually dead but now I am spiritually alive. From death to life is to move from one extreme to another. So it is reasonable to expect a change. A change of belief, of attitude and of behavior will be inevitable if this claim is genuine.

John works all this out for us in his First Epistle. He says if a person is truly born of God there are clear evidences. There will be:—

- a change in belief 5:1
- a change in behavior 2:29; 3:9; 5:18
- a change in attitude 5:4
- a change in relationships 4:7

A new Christian may not understand much doctrine. He may not be able to define justification by faith but he will know and believe with no doubt that Jesus is the Christ. He believes this not just because it is taught to him but because he is born of God. It is the result of being born again. There will also be a change of behavior, and John is keen to emphasize this. The born again man moves in the realm of righteousness not sin. This new standard of behavior is because there has been a change of attitude. The world does not dominate the Christian's thinking. It used to, but now he fights the world's attitudes and because he is born of God he is able more and more to gain victory. Being born again brings the love of God into the center of a person's life and this results in a change of relationships (4:7). These changes John says are the evidences of being born of God and without them we have no right to say that anyone is born again. John is very explicit about this in 3:10, where he says: "This is how we know who the children of God are and who the children of the devil are: Anyone who does not do what is right is not a child of God; nor is anyone who does not love his brother." These signs differentiate the children of God from the children of the devil.

We need to sound *a word of caution* here. These signs do not make themselves known all at once. You would not expect a new born baby to behave like a full grown adult. He will obviously not have the same maturity or understanding. So in a new born again person you do not expect to see the action of a mature Christian, but you do expect to see signs of life.

Take for instance this change of beliefs. In 5:1-5, John is speaking of the nature of faith. This is not an article of faith, this is faith. A Christian believes that Jesus is the Son of God, the Christ, Divine, and he believes this because he is born of God. A new Christian will not have a well developed theology all worked out but *they will* believe this. He must believe this because his whole salvation depends upon it. If Jesus is not divine, then He is no more than a man: if He is no more than a man then He is a sinner: if He is a sinner then He cannot be my Savior: if He

29

is not my Savior then I have no Savior. You see our salvation rests on *who* Jesus is as well as *what* He did on the
cross. But if Jesus is the Son of God, then He is sinless,
and He qualifies to be my Savior. There can be no waver-
ing here, for one of the crucial marks of life seen at once
when a person is born again is this belief in who Jesus is.

The change of behavior comes more gradually but none
the less these are changes immediately after the new birth
occurs. Some Christians have great difficulty with 1John
3:9 which says, "no one who is born of God will continue
in sin. . . . he cannot go on sinning because he is born of
God." This does not mean sinlessness. This is evident
from 1:8-9, where we are told that the Christian will never
claim to be without sin and is urged to confess his sins.
What John means is that the Christian cannot go on in a
life dominated by sin. New life inevitably brings changes
to the life style and pattern. The speed of these changes
will be there. Matthew Henry, the 17th century Bible commentator, was perfectly right when he wrote "if the Gospel
has done nothing for your temper then it has done nothing
for your soul."

A New Born Baby

Let us now, secondly, work out this change by again
paralleling the physical and spiritual births. When a baby
is born certain things happen that show you that all is well
and the baby is healthy. Modern day theologian James
Packer itemizes these when he says the baby cries, sucks,
moves and rests. A baby instinctively *cries*. Is not this

what the mother is eager to hear immediately after the birth? The cry encourages her to believe all is well. So too the born again person cries to God in prayer. The new birth gives the person a new relationship to God and he cannot but delight in it. He cries to his heavenly Father in praises, dependence, hope and trust. Prayer is an evidence of genuine new birth. Not the formal prayers of the religious man but the cries of a child to the Father (Rom. 8:15; Gal. 4:5).

A new born baby *sucks*. He feels a hunger for food and if he does not get it he makes a terrible noise. Peter says the new born Christian has a similar hunger for spiritual food. He listens to the word preached and he reads the Bible regularly. He wants to learn and discuss and question. Why? Because he can't help it. He is spiritually hungry and must be satisfied. If someone who professes faith has no hunger for the Word of God it would be dangerous to say he is born again.

A new born baby *moves*. He turns his head, moves his limbs and later he will crawl and eventually walk. Similarly the new born moves in his new spiritual life. He is eager to explore and discover things and be useful in the service of God. He has to sort out priorities. Spiritual life means spiritual activity.

Finally, the new born baby *rests*. He sleeps a great deal. The new born Christian learns to rest in the Lord. There he finds his strength and sustenance. He learns to say with the Psalmist: "I have stilled and quieted my soul: like a weaned child with its mother" (Ps. 131:2).

These things you do not teach a child. They are instinctive and are signs of life. Spiritual life is far different from nominal religion and is the product only of being born again.

WATER 4 & WIND

We have seen why we must be born again and examined some of the evidences by which it is possible to know if someone is born again. But perhaps the most important question is, *how do we become born again?*

In John 3 Jesus says three times, in verses 5, 6, 8, that being born again means being born of the Spirit. It is to be born from above, in other words it is the work of God. If a person is born again it is as the result of a sovereign activity of God the Holy Spirit. Jesus emphasized this in John 1:12, 13. The new birth means to be born of God.

This is illustrated very clearly in Acts 2 in the narrative of the pouring out of the Holy Spirit upon the church. What was the great and immediate result of the giving of the Holy Spirit in Acts 2? Some say, the greatest thing about Pentecost is tongues (the amazing phenomena when ordinary people began to speak fluently in languages they did not know). Clearly this is important but to say it is the greatest thing at Pentecost is wrong. That would be to put the incidental above the crucial. God did not give the Holy Spirit in order that men might speak in tongues. True, they spoke in tongues because they had been filled with the Spirit, but the main purpose and prime result of Pentecost was that 3000 souls were saved. And that this was no flash in the pan is emphasized by the Lord adding daily to the church those who were being saved (v. 47).

The Holy Spirit was given that the Christians might have the power and authority to preach the Gospel in such a way that people would be brought from spiritual death to spiritual life. In the remainder of Acts tongues is only mentioned twice, whereas we are continually reading of people being saved. This is not surprising because Jesus said in John 16 when the Holy Spirit comes he will convict the world of guilt in regard to sin and righteousness and judgment.

Water

In John 3:5, Jesus tells us how God brings about regeneration. It is by water and the Spirit. Born of water is a phrase used nowhere else in scripture and many different interpretations have been given as to what Jesus meant.

It is important to bear in mind that Jesus is stating here how God brings about the miracle of the new birth. He is telling us what leads up to it, what God uses. That being the case, water cannot here mean baptism. Baptism is a sign of what has taken place, it therefore follows new birth, it does not precede it.

Some say that water refers to the Holy Spirit and quote John 4:4 and 7:37-39. This is clearly a possibility and would mean that Jesus was merely repeating himself in John 3:5 for emphasis. Almost as if Jesus was underlining the absolute necessity of the work of the Spirit in regeneration.

But there is another interpretation that is more satisfactory if we consider v. 5 to be describing God's instruments in bringing about regeneration. In many places in scripture the instrument God uses to bring people to new birth is the Word. Psalm 119:50 (AV) "For Thy word hath quickened me." James 1:18. "He chose to give us birth through the Word of Truth." 1st Peter 1:18-23. "For you have been born again. . . . through the living and enduring word of God." If we also bear in mind that in scripture water is also used as a symbol for the Word (Eph. 5:26) it is not unreasonable to conclude that v. 5 is referring to the fact that the Word of God is also crucial in the new birth.

Wind

In v. 8 Jesus uses the symbol of the wind, and this clearly is meant to illustrate the independence and power of the Holy Spirit. The wind cannot be seen or controlled. Its power is awesome. Trees that have stood for hundreds of years can suddenly in a moment be torn up by the power of the wind. The wind acts in its own sovereign way and all we can do is to feel its influence and see its effects. Jesus

brings these truths before us and says, so it is with everyone born of the Spirit. The Holy Spirit works in his own
sovereign and almighty way to bring about new birth. The
Spirit cannot be manipulated or controlled. He works when
and where he wills with an awesome majesty and irresist-
ible power.

What a shock this is to those who believe they can save
themselves by their own efforts and by man-made religion.
Salvation by our own works must be the greatest delusion
the Devil has ever imposed upon mankind. To think we
can achieve by our own efforts what Jesus says only the
mighty power of the Holy Spirit can do, is arrogance and
foolishness beyond belief.

What a lesson there is in the illustration of the wind for
the person who knows he needs to be born again but continually argues, "not now, I will leave it a few years." The
truth is we can no more pick the day of our new birth than
we could our physical birth. The Holy Spirit is sovereign
in being born again. Here is something most humbling to
proud, self-sufficient men and women. And yet this truth
is most encouraging to some poor soul that feels so weak
and sinful and helpless, but longs to be right with God.
God is the author of salvation. He does it all. The wind
blows where it pleases. Trust me, says God. I will save.

The Day of Pentecost

Let us now see how God uses water and wind, the Word
and the Spirit in the new birth - this work of God that is so
radical and devastating, that takes a soul dead in sin and

makes it alive in God: that takes a sinner from condemnation to acceptance with God. All this is clearly illustrated in Acts 2 on the Day of Pentecost, as God brings about the salvation of 3000 people.

Firstly, God brings men and women to hear the Gospel. They have to be born of water, of the Word, so they need to hear the Word of God. Paul says that faith comes by hearing the Word of God (Rom. 10:17). We are living in days when the vast majority of people never read the Bible and never hear the Gospel preached. And so it was in the first century. These 3000 saved at Pentecost were Jews. They had the scriptures but they did not understand them and they had never heard the Gospel of Jesus Christ.

But they must hear, so God the Holy Spirit makes this possible. In Acts 2, he uses the strange phenomena of the violent wind and tongues (see v. 6) to gather the crowd together. The tongues they heard were not meaningless babble, but the declaration of the wonders of God (v. 11). Then when the crowd was gathered, Peter preached the Gospel to them. It was all the work of the Spirit to enable the people to hear the Word.

It is still the same. God will use various means to bring sinners to hear the Word. It may be we were born into a Christian family and always go to church, but most folk are not. How are they to hear? God will use circumstances of a funeral or a wedding, the witness of Christian friends, a casual hearing at an open air meeting, a tract through the door. The list is endless but if a sinner is to be saved, he *must* hear the Word of God.

Sinners need to hear this Gospel and all the essential ingredients of Gospel preaching are found in Peter's sermon on Pentecost.

God's sovereign purposes (v. 16)

The person and work of Jesus (vv. 22-24)

Man's sin and guilt (vv. 23,26)

The call to repentance (v. 38)

There is only one Gospel and this is it.

Secondly, while hearing the Gospel is crucial to new birth, it is not enough. So now the Holy Spirit begins to work on these hearers of the Word. When the people saw the signs and wonders it produced two groups - in v. 12 there are honest inquirers and in v. 13 those who ridiculed the whole thing. But when the Word is preached in the power of the Holy Spirit, a third group emerges out of these two. There are those now who receive the Word in faith and repentance (v. 41).

These folk came to this position because the Holy Spirit took the Word preached and by it convicted them of their sin. So we read in v. 37, that what they heard cut them to the heart. The Word made a deep and devastating impression upon them, and it did so because of the power and influence of the Holy Spirit. Many people go to a church where the Gospel is preached but they never understand what they hear. Many do not listen, as soon as the text is announced they switch off. This is the natural man's response to the Gospel, so a man may hear the Gospel a hundred times and it bounces off him like a rubber ball off a stone wall. But when the Holy Spirit is at work the reaction is different. People listen. They see their own sin and guilt. They are convicted and cry out, "What must we do?"

The water and the wind, the Word and the Spirit alone can bring a sinner to this position. And the answer to the convicted sinner's cry is always the same, repent. At Pentecost 3000 sinners were born again, they found mercy and pardon in Christ and came to the Savior in repentance and faith. What Nicodemus thought to be impossible ("How can this be?", he asked) became the joyous experience of these 3000 and of countless millions down to our day. How can a man be born when he is old, was his other incredulous question, and the answer, as many old age pensioners have found, is through the Word and the Spirit.

CHRIST LIFTED UP

Nicodemus was an intelligent, religious man and one very familiar with the Old Testament. He came to Jesus because he was anxious to learn from Him. As a Pharisee this was a very unusual attitude but Nicodemus recognized the truth of what was being said about Jesus, that no man spoke with the authority of this man. This was no exaggeration because Jesus was undoubtedly the greatest teacher the world has ever known. So in John 3, we have the meeting of the greatest teacher and the intelligent man who wants to learn, yet Nicodemus could not make heads or tails of what Jesus was saying. His reaction to the teaching of Jesus was, how can this be?

Why could he not understand? Jesus alludes to the answer in v. 10, "You are Israel's teacher, and do you not understand these things?" Nicodemus was a theological expert, a man well versed in the Old Testament literature and history. Therefore you would expect him to understand Jesus, but in fact his religious background was an obstacle to spiritual understanding. Nicodemus was brought up as a Pharisee with certain preconceived doctrines that he obviously accepted as true, so that when he was confronted with the Truth as it is in Jesus, his religious beliefs got in the way of true belief.

It must have been very hard for this Pharisee to unlearn all that he had always believed. Unlearning is much more difficult than learning and that is why there are few obstacles more of a hindrance to true faith than religion. Religion colors our thinking about God. It does not matter if the religion is Islam or Hinduism or the 101 varieties of Christianity available today. They set in our minds certain concepts about God that are unbiblical, so that when the religious man is faced with biblical truths he often reacts with antagonism. For instance, if a man is brought up on a doctrine that teaches all you need to be a Christian is to be kind and respectable and go to church occasionally, and this man is told that like everyone else he is a sinner and needs to be born again, it comes as a shock and his inevitable reaction is to reject it. There is no one who will react so strongly against the biblical accusation that all men and women are sinners under the judgment and wrath of God, as the religious man. To be told that there is no difference in the sight of God between the terrorist killer and the religious man who is not born again is sure to cause anger and resentment.

So Nicodemus could not understand because of a spiritual blindness that was encouraged by his religion. But

Jesus is infinitely patient and he speaks now in terms that Nicodemus ought to be able to understand. He takes the Pharisee back to Numbers chapter 21 and a familiar story that he would know as a fact of history. It is a story that he would have read many times but Jesus explains it in the most glorious spiritual way - "just as Moses lifted up the snake in the desert, so the Son of Man must be lifted up, that everyone who believes in Him may have eternal life" (Jn. 3:14).

The Bronze Snake

The story in Numbers 21 tells of the rebellion of the people of Israel against God. They were in the wilderness under the judgment of God because of a previous rebellion, but God was good to them and gave them water from the rock and provided daily food in the form of manna, a kind of honey wafer. But they were impatient and complained against God, and in this frame of mind they easily exaggerated their problem. There is no water, they said, but of course there was, and with regard to the manna, they said, we detest this miserable food.

God dealt with this sin, and notice in Numbers 21:6, God *sent* poisonous snakes among them. The snakes were no accident. It was no piece of bad luck that they happened to camp at the spot where the snakes were. This was God's judgment - they were God sent. Many Israelites died and at last the people realized that it was because of their sin. They turned to Moses to mediate with God for them. God in his mercy answered Moses' prayer and though he did not remove the snakes he provided an answer. Moses was to make a bronze snake and put it on a pole so that everyone could see it. If any one was bitten by a snake and its poison was beginning to do its deadly work, if they looked to that provision of God's grace, the bronze snake, they would not die but live.

That was the story. Now Jesus says even as Moses did that, so too must He, the Son of Man be lifted up. What did Jesus mean by his being lifted up? We do not have to guess because we are told in John 12:32-33, that this was a reference to his death. So Jesus is talking about his death on the Cross and he is saying that the action of Moses illustrates perfectly how Jesus saves men from their sin and gives them new life.

Rebellion & It's Consequences

The story of the bronze snake starts in Numbers 21:4-5 with the people rebelling against God. They do not want to go God's way. They want their own way, and they find the gifts and provisions of God detestable. They become sick of what God gives them, so they rebel. They do not want God to rule them. They sin, for this is what sin is, it is a rejection of the authority and will of God. Every time we sin, no matter what the sin is, we are in fact rejecting God's way and going our own way. We are saying that the things of God are not good for us, and that we know better.

That is the state of all of us naturally. That is why we find prayer so boring and the Bible so irrelevant. These provisions of God's grace are as detestable to the ordinary man as the manna was to the Israelites. So they sin.

Sin is very easy but it always brings its consequences, and did for these Israelites. The Lord sent judgment. God is holy and he cannot and will not tolerate sin. At the beginning of his dealing with man, God said to Adam if you sin you will die (Genesis 2:17). So divine judgment comes via the snakes and people die.

God's dealing with us today may not be identical to the Israelites in the Old Testament, but in effect it is the same. When we sin, we do not expect to get bitten by a snake but that sin will still bring its consequence. The wages of sin is still death and every town in the country has its monuments to this fact. We call them cemeteries. Why will we all die one day? A doctor will examine our dead bodies and will enter on the death certificate the cause of death. He may write cancer, or heart attack or pneumonia, or whatever it is, but he will be wrong. These are not the *real* cause of death, they are merely the means by which death comes to us. The cause is sin. Why did those Israelites die in the desert? Because they were bitten by snakes? No! They died because they sinned.

God's Answer

If this reality of death as the judgment on sin is true, the vital question has to be, is there an answer? Is there any way guilty sinners can escape this inevitable judgment? God alone provides an answer. His answer is not religion.

God's answer to his own judgment upon sin is Jesus, and this is why Jesus says, he must be lifted up so that everyone who believes in him may have eternal life.

In Numbers 21 we see how God answered the desperate need of the people. It starts in v. 7, when the people said, "we have sinned." There was a confession of guilt and by implication there was repentance. They did not pretend everything was alright. They did not protest their innocence. Neither did they reluctantly acknowledge their sin but protest that God's judgment was too harsh. There was simply a confession of sin and guilt and a plea for mercy. It was then that God provided his answer.

There is no salvation without repentance, and there can be no repentance without conviction of sin. Have you ever said, "I have sinned," and said it with a seriousness and earnestness that anxiously looks for an answer?

God's answer was a very strange one. Moses was to make a model of a snake and put it on a pole. Those in need of God's mercy were to look to this bronze snake and they would live. It was a very strange answer but it was the only one. God did not give them an alternative. This was the only remedy. The same principle is true for us. God's only answer to our sin and guilt is Jesus lifted up on the Cross. On the Cross Jesus died to deal with sin. He died as our Substitute. He died the Just for the unjust. He bore our sins in his body on the Cross. God laid on him all our sin and guilt and Jesus became the Scapegoat, that is, the innocent taking away the sin of the guilty. This is the clear language of the Old and New Testaments to describe what happened when Jesus was lifted up on the Cross.

The command of God to the Israelites in the desert was, look to my provision of love and mercy and live. Likewise the command of the Gospel to guilty sinners is, Look to Jesus, Believe in him as your sin bearer and Savior, and Live. The scripture here does not say so, but human nature being what it is, we can reasonably deduce that some of those bitten by the snakes looked and lived, and others refused. They would argue, "this is nonsense. How can looking to the bronze snake possibly get rid of the poison in my body. This is ridiculous, unreasonable, irrational." Just like Nicodemus, they were saying how can this be? So they would not look and they died. There they lay in the dust of the desert, reasonable, rational and sensible but dead!

Of course, they were not really reasonable, rational and sensible, they were stubborn and above all they were continuing in their rejection of God's way. The bronze serpent was God's only way to avoid physical death and Jesus is God's only way to avoid spiritual death. To look to Jesus means to believe. It means to turn as a guilty, hell deserving sinner to God's provision of grace and mercy. Those folk in Numbers 21 knew they were dying and they knew why. Their only alternative to death was to look to the bronze snake. Those who did, lived.

Death is the wages of sin. We are all sinners and therefore we will all die, and this does not mean only the death of the body but the eternal judgment of God in hell. The only answer to this awful state is God's answer. Jesus said he was to be lifted up on the cross so that everyone who believes in him may have eternal life.

GOD
SO LOVED
THE WORLD

John 3:16 is probably the most well known verse in the Bible and has been described as the Gospel in a nutshell, or the most perfect summary of the Gospel. This is no overstatement because every truth that a sinner needs to be saved is contained in these words of Jesus - "For God so loved the world that He gave His only begotten Son, that whoever believes in Him shall not perish but have eternal life."

The Gospel starts with an activity of God and leads on to demand a response from man. The order is important. Man is called upon to respond to an action of God. The initiative is God's. If God had done nothing to save us, then we could do nothing. We are so used to thinking of life and society in terms of the activity of man that we find this difficult to accept. Man as the master of his own des-

tiny is a precious belief, yet in so many areas of life it is
just not true. Ask the millions who go to bed hungry every
night if they are masters of their own destiny. Ask the pris-
oners in a hijacked plane threatened with death by terror-
ists. In so many areas of life we are not in control of our
own destiny but caught up and subject to forces and pres-
sures, conditions and circumstances beyond our control.

Nowhere is this more true than in the spiritual realm
and the affairs of our immortal souls. Of man as a spiritual
being, Jesus says some very important things in John 3.
He says in v. 18 that the sinner is condemned already. That
means we are condemned by God and as a consequence
we will perish, and perish means eternal judgment in hell.
Jesus is saying this, not some wild-eyed fanatical preacher.
And He is not speculating upon what may or may not be,
but stating what He the Son of God knows to be true and
certain. In vv. 5 & 6, Jesus went even further and said there
is nothing we can do about this terrible condition. This is
so because of the nature of sin. Man is a sinner, and sin
enslaves, dominates, and controls.

It is to this very real problem that the Gospel addresses
itself. It addresses itself to men where they are. It does not
pretend that they are anything but sinners. Man has always found great difficulty accepting this prime biblical
concept and consequently while they recognize the symp-
tom of sin and seek to deal with those, they never acknowledge the root cause which is man's nature and alienation
from God. Sin is the problem and only the Gospel has the
answer to it because the Gospel spells out the activity of
God in dealing with this massive problem.

God's answer to sin is that He so loved the world that he gave his one and only begotten Son. This is a statement of tremendous significance and of amazing content and consequence.

World

That God should love Jesus is perfectly understandable. Twice in the New Testament God broke the silence of eternity and shouted down from heaven, "This is my beloved Son" (Matt. 3:17; 17:5). The whole life of Jesus was lived in absolute obedience to the will and word of God, so it is understandable that God should love him. We could even say it is understandable that God should love certain men like Moses and David, who in spite of many failures, tried to serve and obey him. But that God should love the world is amazing when you consider that by and large most people in the world have no time for God. There is no love or respect for God, only resentment and blatant opposition. Blasphemy is considered by many to be normal and acceptable, God an irrelevance. Yet God still loves the world, and as John Calvin put it, "Although there is nothing in the world deserving God's favor, He nevertheless shows He is favorable to the whole world when He calls all without exception to faith in Christ".[5]

As we all consider our past reaction and attitude to God and His Gospel, do we honestly believe that we deserve this divine love? Of course not, yet God loves us.

It is not that God loved the world but that He *so* loved.

The little word "so" immediately confronts us with something exceptional and extraordinary. That God should love the world is amazing but that He should do it in the way He did is beyond comprehension. This love was not a general sort of benevolence but a particular act - He gave His only begotten Son. We have seen from v. 14 & 15 that this means, God gave Jesus to die on the Cross in place of guilty sinners. This leads us to note three things about God's love for the world.

Undeserved Love

Paul describes the undeserved nature of God's love for us in the lovely words of Romans 5:6-8, "You see, at just the right time, when we were still powerless, Christ died for the ungodly. Very rarely will anyone die for a righteous man, though for a good man someone might possibly dare to die. But God demonstrates His own love for us in this: While we were still sinners, Christ died for us". God shows love to the ungodly. Ungodly means unlike God. Man was made in the image of God but sin has so disfigured this image that man is now ungodly. He does not love God or know God; he is, says the Bible, an enemy of God, alien and hostile, at war with God.

The greatest thing about man, as distinct from all other created beings, is not his brain, but that he was made to know and enjoy God. Sin has robbed us of that. We have no rights nor claims. Man is in a hopeless position but the Gospel says, Christ died for the ungodly because God loves sinners, who do not, indeed cannot deserve it!

FROM RELIGION TO CHRIST

Unsought Love

John in his first epistle, chapter 4 verse 10, brings before us this staggering description of divine love "This is love: not that we loved God, but that he loved us and sent his Son as an atoning sacrifice for our sins".

Ungodly man does not love God, nor seek to be loved by God. Man's nature and mind are so darkened by sin that he is ignorant of God's love and mercy. He takes the blessings of life for granted– health, food, breath, the beauty of creation are never acknowledged as gifts of God. We talk about Mother Nature, while the Bible talks about the Creator God. We talk about the Laws of Nature, while the Bible talks about the will and providence of God. Because we exclude God we do not seek Him. *But He seeks us!* In Jesus, God came to seek and save the lost. It was not that we loved Him but He loved us. And what a love! Divine love is not an empty, sentimental pity but it demonstrates itself in an act of propitiation.

Propitiation being the word the NIV bible translates as *atoning sacrifice* and means that on the cross, bearing our sin and guilt, Jesus endured the wrath of God *instead* of us, and paid fully on our behalf the debt we owed to God for breaking His holy law. On the cross our Savior cried, "My God, my God why have You forsaken Me?" (Matthew 27:46). The Holy God forsook His Son because He was our sin-bearer - "God made Him who had no sin to be sin for us" (2 Corinthians 5:21). Jesus was "stricken by

50

God, smitten by Him, and afflicted" (Isaiah 53:4). On the cross the Old Testament prophecy of Zechariah 13:7 was being fulfilled: "'Awake, O sword, against my shepherd. . .' declares the Lord Almighty. "Strike the shepherd. . .'". The sword was the sword of judgment, and in Matthew 26:31 Jesus tells us clearly that this verse speaks of Him.

In other words, at Calvary our Lord made it possible for a holy God to pardon us even though we were sinners and had broken His holy law. God dealt with the problem of sin in the only way that could satisfy His holy justice and enable Him to move in and break the power of Satan in the lives of lost sinners. Specifically by punishing the only man that qualified to be our substitute by virtue of His sinlessness, and the only man who could after enduring the wrath of God equivalent to our being in Hell for all eternity, take up His own life again and rise from the grave, that is a man who was also God Himself.

Unimaginable Love

"How great is the love that the Father has lavished upon us", 1 John 3:1.

The word lavished is an extravagant word depicting something overloaded, extreme. Lavished speaks of abundance, and tells us that God's love is no small, carefully measured thing, but a love unimaginable in its beauty and bounty. It is this lavished love that enables God to give his Son for us. Who would ever imagine God doing such a thing for miserable hell deserving sinners?

51

How is it possible to describe such love? The hymn writer talks of love, vast as the ocean, loving kindness as deep as the flood. The deep, deep love of Jesus is vast, unmeasured, boundless and free.

The Gospel finds us dead in sin, helpless in its all consuming power, and offers us this unimaginable love. Many people say, "I do not feel dead and helpless." Sadly that is true of many and that is why they have never gasped in amazement at this love of God, undeserved, unsought and unimaginable.

WHOEVER

From the heart of God there comes to all men and women, whoever we are and whatever we are, this wondrous love. "God so loved the world...". God loves us so much that He not only allowed Jesus to die instead of us but He planned it. Isaiah the Prophet says, "it was the Lord's will to crush Him and cause Him to suffer" (Isaiah 53:10). That is love. No one has ever loved us like that and no one ever could. This is love divine, all loves excelling.

This love becomes even more radiant when we appreciate who it is that God loves. He loves the world, but when God looks down from heaven upon mankind, what does he see? Psalm 14:2, 3 answers this question for us - "The Lord looks down from heaven on the sons of men to see if there are any who understand, any who seek God. All have turned aside, they have together become corrupt, there is no one who does good not even one." This is a devastating criticism of mankind - All have turned aside, all are corrupt, there is no one who does good. There are no exceptions. Holiness and justice would demand that such guilty creatures should receive everlasting damnation. That is what the word perish means in John 3:16. This is what God's justice *demands* but his love says, NO. God loves His people and He will satisfy the just demands of His own law by imputing their sin and guilt to His sinless Son, and by punishing those sins borne by Jesus. So Jesus dies on behalf of sinners, to make atonement for their sin. Love produces salvation. God's holiness makes the cross necessary but it is God's love that makes it possible.

This then is what God has done, and in the proclamation of the Gospel God demands a response from us. The response God wants is to be found in the words, "whoever believes in Him."

No Boundaries

"Whoever" is a big word, an encouraging word, a word full of hope and potential. Like the word "world" it is all embracing. Jesus obviously used this word very deliberately. Calvin said, "He has employed the universal term whosoever, both to invite all indiscriminately to partake of life, and to cut off every excuse from unbelievers." 'Whoever' removes every excuse a sinner may have for not coming to the Savior. Never will a man appear in the day of the revelation of the righteous judgment of God who will be able to say that he longed and desired and willed, and sought earnestly to come, but was refused.

Whoever

For many reasons people seek to put a boundary upon God's love. Nicodemus as a Pharisee would have done so. To the Pharisees God's love was for the Jews only and not for the Gentiles. "Whoever" shatters that Jewish illusion.

Some folk say, "my life is so rotten that God could not love me. I am so wicked that there can be no hope for me." Sometimes Christians do the same thing and see some types of people beyond redemption.

'Whoever' shatters this myth.

Others argue "what about the doctrine of election?". Does not the Bible teach that only the elect will be saved? Yes it does but as John Brown[6] strongly argues in his book *Discourses and Sayings of our Lord*, - "the revelation of mercy made in the Gospel, refers to men as sinners, not as elect sinners! The invitations and promises of the Gospel calling upon men to believe in Jesus are addressed to all, and are true and applicable to all without exception". So Brown says "I am persuaded that the doctrine of personal election is very plainly taught in Scripture; but I am equally persuaded that the minister misunderstands that doctrine who finds it, in the least degree, hampering him in presenting a full and a free salvation as the gift of God to every one who hears the Gospel; and that the man abuses the doctrine who finds in it anything which operates as a barrier in the way of his receiving, as a sinner, all the blessings of the Christian salvation, in the belief of the truth. Indeed, when rightly understood, it can have no such effect."

'Whoever' leaves us all without an excuse because, to quote John Brown again, "in consequence of that atonement, every sinner may be, and if he believes in Jesus certainly shall be, pardoned and saved."

Here is the glory of the word whoever. No one can ever say, the Gospel has nothing to say to me. Whoever means you, me, everyone. The Gospel addresses itself to all as the following Bible verses make very clear:-

"The Spirit and the bride say, "Come!" And let him who hears say, "Come!" Whoever is thirsty, let him come; and whoever wishes, let him take the free gift of the water of life" (Rev. 22:17).

"Come, all you who are thirsty, come to the waters, and you who have no money, come, buy and eat! Come, buy wine and milk, without money and without cost. Why spend money on what is not bread, and your labor on what does not satisfy? Listen, listen to me, and eat what is good, and your soul will delight in the richest of fare. Give ear and come to me; hear me, that your soul may live. I will make an everlasting covenant with you, my faithful love promised to David" (Isaiah 55:1-3).

"Say to them, As surely as I live, declares the Sovereign Lord, I take no pleasure in the death of the wicked, but rather that they turn from their ways and live. Turn. Turn from your evil ways! Why will you die, O house of Israel?" (Eze. 33:11).

'Whoever' is such an encouragement to us all but it is also a frightening word because it leaves the sinner without excuse. No one will be able to appear before God on the day of judgment and say he longed to be saved, and sought earnestly for salvation but was refused. No, says the Bible, whoever believes will be saved. Jesus has promised in John 6:37 "Whoever comes to me I will never drive away."

The Drawing of God

If there are no boundaries to God's love, why is it that men will not come to Jesus? After the promise of John 6:37, Jesus goes on to say in v. 44 "no one can come to me unless the Father who sent me draws him." Once more we are back to why it is crucial that we be born again. No one can come to Jesus because the power of sin renders them helpless. They are dead in sin and dead men can do nothing. Left to themselves sinners will not come to God because they cannot. They need to be drawn and in the next verse Jesus explains what this means, "everyone who listens to the Father and learns from him comes to me."

Drawing is the work of the Holy Spirit through the preaching of the Gospel. To souls dead in sin, God begins to speak. The Holy Spirit convicts of sin and gives the gift of faith which leads to repentance. It is not an emotional experience in church, though it can be part of it. The mind as well as the emotions are involved. The sinner listens and learns from the Father, said Jesus. This can take place in a matter of minutes and some folk are converted the first time they hear the Gospel, but for most of us it occurs over a period of days or weeks or even years. We have heard the Gospel and we begin to understand. What was previously dull and boring becomes riveting and absorbing. We find that when we are washing the dishes, or driving the car, or doing our daily work that our mind suddenly turns to God. We want God and we cannot get rid of the longing. It may come and go, but it does not go very far. We do not like the conviction of sin which we feel and may vow never to go to church again, but we do. Why? Because God is drawing. We find ourselves uncertain where previously we were very sure. We knew the Bible was full of myths but now we are not so sure. We are being taught of God and its all part of his drawing.

Belief

If God is drawing, what is it that God wants that person to do? Jesus tells us in John 3:16. He wants us to believe in Jesus.

Belief in the Bible is not just an intellectual response of the mind. The heart too must be involved. In Romans 10:10 Paul says, "for it is with your heart that you believe and are justified." Believing in the mind, that is accepting the truth concerning the facts of the Gospel, is crucial but it is not enough. James said even the devils believe in this way (Jas. 2:19). In Romans 10, Paul is not talking of a superficial confession accompanied by no more than a token faith. Belief in the heart refers to a faith that takes hold of the whole inner man.

INTELLECT: This means we believe the facts. We believe Jesus was born of the Virgin. We believe in His Deity and sinlessness. We believe He died for sinners and that God raised Him from the Dead.

EMOTIONS: Our belief is not a cold, matter of fact belief but it moves us. True belief will both thrill and frighten. We are thrilled to think God loves us and frightened to think of the consequence of not having Jesus as our Savior.

WILL:You act upon what you believe. Your belief causes you to flee in faith and repentance to Jesus.

All this is included in what it means to believe in Jesus. To believe means to have faith in Jesus. There is an old Sunday School acrostic that explains what faith means.

FORSAKING ALL I TAKE HIM.

If you believe intellectually and your emotions are stirred by the Gospel then turn now to Jesus for forgiveness of sin. You are being drawn by God, so come to Jesus and come with this guarantee of Jesus, "whoever comes to Me I will not drive away."

DEATH
OR
LIFE

In John 3:16 we have seen the action of God and the response of man. This order is important. If God had not loved us and given Jesus to die for us there could be nothing for us to respond to. We look now at the problem the Gospel seeks to erase and its ultimate achievement. This is all summed up in the words perish and everlasting life.

Perish

The great purpose of the Gospel is to prevent men and women from perishing. What does perish mean and why do we perish? The answer to why, is clear from the passage. It is the result of sin. This is seen in the illustration of Moses and the snake. Why did the Israelites die in the desert? Because they were bitten by snakes? No. It was because they had sinned, (the snakes were simply God's means of bring death). This truth is further expounded by Jesus in John 3:19. Men love darkness because their deeds are evil. Death or perishing is God's judgment upon human sin. God made this very clear before a single sin had been committed - "You must not eat from the tree of the knowledge of good or evil, for when you eat of it you will surely die" (Genesis 2:17).

So perishing means death which is the certain result of sin. It is the judgment of God's holy wrath upon sin. Paul spells it out for us in Romans 5:12, "Therefore, just as sin entered the world through one man, and death through sin, and in this way death came to all men, because all sinned". This is the awful truth but we cannot leave it there. Perish or death in John 3:16 is the opposite to eternal life. Not the opposite of life, but to eternal life. This is very important because all the sects and many nominal Christians say death means the end of conscious existence or annihilation and therefore there is no hell. They all reject the concept of eternal conscious punishment in hell. But the context shows that perish means far more than losing physical existence. Sin is a spiritual problem and its condemnation is a spiritual as well as a judicial act of God. Therefore its punishment is also spiritual and not merely physical.

The perishing in John 3:16 indicates divine condemnation, complete and everlasting, so that the guilty sinner is banned from the presence and love of God and dwells forever in the presence of the wrath of God. Annihilation is obviously to be separated from the love of God but it ignores the New Testament teaching of the eternal wrath of God (see Matthew 25:41, 46; Luke 16:22-26).

The Bible uses picture language to describe hell but what is clear is that the fires of hell are the wrath of the holy God. It is the awfulness of sin that makes hell necessary but it is the holiness of God that creates hell. Hell is to be exposed without a Savior, to the holiness of God for all eternity (see 2 Thessalonians 1:6-9; Hebrews 10:27-31). In the New Testament it is Jesus who speaks mostly about hell and he has some terrible things to say about it, but by far the most terrible word that the Savior used about hell is, eternal. Hell is as eternal as heaven. There is no end to it. In life, even in the darkest moments, there is always the hope that things will get better. There is no such hope in hell. Souls are lost forever. Listen to Charles Spurgeon,[7] "On every chain in hell is written - forever. If I could tell you that one day the fires of hell will burn out and that the lost might be saved, then there would be rejoicing in hell at the very thought - but it cannot be so; forever damned, forever cast into outer darkness".

That is what it means to perish and Jesus came to save us from that.

Eternal Life

The adjective *everlasting* or *eternal* is used seventeen times in John's Gospel and always with the noun, life. It speaks of a quality of life - "Now this is eternal life; that they may know you, the only true God, and Jesus Christ, whom you have sent" (17:3). But it also speaks of duration of life, it is never ending. Eternal life starts not at death but at new birth. It starts when we know God. It is a quality of life experienced now, that is altogether different from life under the dominion of sin, and it is a foretaste, in a limited way, of heaven.

Heaven is the eternal dwelling place of all those who have been born again. It is a place where there is no sin, no pain, no suffering, because there the rule of God's righteousness is complete and unchallenged. There we shall be free from the corruption of human nature. There we shall see Jesus face to face and be like him, not equal to him but like him in that sin will not dominate us. Everlasting life is everlasting happiness without the slightest shadow or blemish to it. And for a being like man, who was made *in the image of God*, made *by God* and *for God*, such happiness *must* consist in *knowing God* without any hindrance from sin. John Brown said it will mean, "Having our mind conformed to his mind, our wishes subjected to his pleasure, thinking along with him, willing along with him, choosing what he chooses, seeking and finding enjoyment in what he finds enjoyment. This is life. This is happiness. And the never ending continuance of this is everlasting life."

To know God transforms a person and introduces him to a life he could not otherwise experience. To know God is to have eternal life and this is what the Gospel seeks to give us. God loved us for this purpose. God gave his Son to die on the Cross so that we may know this. The Gospel is great because its Author is great, its subject is great, its gift is great and its achievement is great - that sinners should not perish but have eternal life in the Lord Jesus Christ.

The situation the Gospel addresses itself to is not a pleasant one. Souls perishing and going to hell is not pleasant but it is the truth and the Gospel is concerned with truth.

Many people object strenuously to the preaching of hell. Hell-fire preaching today is a term of scorn and amusement but the fact is that the New Testament speaks of this terrible place and for us to pretend that it does not exist or remain silent on the subject is to do the greatest possible disservice to sinful mankind. Several years ago a city in the United States was concerned about the noise level on its streets and they decided to ban the use of car horns. The harsh noisy sound was silenced but after a while they discovered there was a sharp rise of deaths on the city roads and they had to bring back the car horns. The horn is a harsh, noisy intrusion but it is a necessary warning and it saves lives. The preaching of hell likewise is a serious warning to sinners and the Gospel has no hesitation about declaring it because the Gospel has the answer to this terrible truth. To preach hell and not at the same time to preach God's answer to it is to preach something that is not the Gospel. The Gospel says men need *not* perish because Jesus has conquered sin, death and hell. Listen to Paul's great shout of praise in 1 Corinthians 15:55-57 "Where, O death, is your sting? Where, O Hades (grave), is your victory? The sting of death is sin, and the power of sin is the law. But thanks be to God! He gives us the victory through our Lord Jesus Christ."

The Gospel answer to sin and hell is that, "God so loved the world that He gave His one and only Son, that whoever believes in Him shall not perish but have eternal life."

THE SIN OF UNBELIEF

Why did God send Jesus into the world? In verse 17 Jesus answers this in the negative, it was not to condemn the world. He answered this way because he was speaking to Nicodemus the Pharisee, a man steeped in Jewish tradition. One of these traditions was that the Messiah would come to punish the world, and world for them meant all nations except the Jews. They thought God loved them and hated all other people. Jesus flatly contradicts this. He said God loved the world and God sending his Son was a display of love on God's part to the human race.

In verse 18 Jesus makes the point that the world was condemned long before God sent his Son into it. Jesus came to a world that was already under the wrath and judgment of God. It is a world of men and women, Jew and Gentile, who are alien to God. People who are by nature children of wrath because of their unbelief and rejection of

God. In this verse Jesus confronts us with the worst sin that any human being can commit. It is not murder, or adultery, or theft, or lies, it is the sin of unbelief. Jesus said in Mark 3:28, 29 "I tell you the truth, all the sins and blasphemies of men will be forgiven them. But whoever blasphemes against the Holy Spirit will never be forgiven; he is guilty of an eternal sin." What is this unforgivable sin? J. C. Ryle says, "The most probable view is, that it is a combination of clear intellectual knowledge of the Gospel with a deliberate rejection of it, and willful choice of sin."

Unbelief is the worst sin for several reasons. Whereas most of our sins are directed at man and indirectly at God, unbelief is a sin directly against God. It does not involve man. When a man rejects the Gospel of the grace of God in the Lord Jesus Christ, he is not merely rejecting the views of a preacher or the doctrines of a church, he is rejecting God. Unbelief makes a mockery of God's greatest work - salvation, and spurns some of God's greatest attributes - love and mercy. David makes it clear in Psalm 51:4 that all sin is against God but unbelief is a sin not only against the word and law of God but against the very character and nature of God.

It is one of the most deceitful of sins because most people do not see anything wrong with it. We would be appalled if one of our family or friends committed murder. We would be ashamed if one of our family was a thief or criminal, and if a friend continually told us lies we would shun him. But if family or friends reject the Gospel we hardly raise an eyebrow. We say it does not matter what a person believes so long as they are sincere and honest.

Nonsense, said Jesus. If a man does not believe in Christ as God's appointed Savior then he stands condemned already by Almighty God.

This is so important that we need to understand the nature of unbelief. Why is it that when God says something so clearly men reject it? The main reason is given in verses 19 - 21 which we shall consider in the next chapter, but now we shall look at unbelief in its two main guises, namely blatant unbelief and disguised unbelief.

Blatant Unbelief

There are people who are determined never to believe God. They say they will never become a Christian, and the reasons for such blatant unbelief are varied.[8]

It may be a person has had a bad experience of Christians. Perhaps they had parents who tried to ram Christianity down their throats, or a father who was one thing in church and something totally different in the home. Perhaps they see hypocrisy in a Christian friend or neighbor, and on the basis of such things they dismiss all Christianity; they dismiss God and Christ. To a degree you can sympathize with these folk, but really it is a totally illogical position. Are we to dismiss all books ever written because some are pornographic? Do we reject every shopkeeper because some may cheat? Do we decide never to fly in a plane because of an isolated crash?

Then there is the blatant unbelief that is based on intellect. It dismisses the Christian faith as intellectual rubbish. This viewpoint assumes that Christianity is so lacking in factual evidence and credibility that no thinking person could possibly believe it. Take for instance the following statement made in print by an unbeliever, "evolution is unproved and unprovable. We believe it only because the only alternative is special creation which is unthinkable." Here is a blatant refusal even to consider the possibility of a Creator. One is tempted to conclude that it is not Christians who should be charged with violence against the intellect! Blatant unbelief clothes the sin of unbelief with a veneer of intellectual respectability but chooses to ignore the fact that some of the greatest minds the world has known like Michael Faraday, Sir John Fleming and James Clerk Maxwell, were Bible believing Christians.[9] The truth of the matter is that whether a man is a university Professor or a road sweeper has nothing to do with whether or not he is a Christian.

Disguised Unbeleief

This is the sort of unbelief characterized by a man like Nicodemus. It is belief in God that disguises an unbelief of God. Nicodemus like all Pharisees believed in God. He knew there was a God and tried to serve and worship Him. The Pharisees were enthusiastic in their religion but when God spoke clearly and distinctly through the scriptures and particularly through Jesus, they rejected it. They did not believe God.

One reason for believing in God but not believing God is that we come to God with all sorts of preconceived ideas and prejudices. The Pharisees were full of this. They believed God loved the Jews and hated the world. They believed the Messiah would be a political, military figure who would bring a national redemption to the Jews. These preconceived beliefs caused them to reject Jesus and we are no different today. We also have our preconceived beliefs. We believe God is love, which is gloriously true, but then we go on to reject any notion of divine judgment. We believe God only expects us to do our best and ignore the fact that his word says all our righteousness is as filthy rags to Him (Isa. 64:7). We believe all religions lead to God and in effect call Jesus a bigoted liar for saying that He alone is the way to God and no one can come to the Father except through Him (Jn. 14:6).

There are many people who believe in God but they will not believe what God says in His Word. Unbelief hides under a guise of religious belief. But God is not deceived.

Jesus clearly puts prime importance upon believing God. As well as these verses we are considering in John 3, look closely at John 5:24; 6:35; 20:31.

When the Gospel comes to a man it finds him already a sinner under the wrath and judgment of the Holy God. The Gospel presents to this man a full and free pardon that can only be received as the sinner believes in the truth of God as found in Jesus. The sinner is condemned not only because of his depraved nature but also, as John 3:18 says so emphatically, because he rejects the Gospel and will not believe in Jesus. He tramples underfoot the authority of Almighty God manifested in the command to believe and repent. He spurns the grace of God as revealed in God not sparing His own Son but giving Him to die for us.

Do you see the finality of unbelief? Our sinful nature from birth condemns us before God but God in Christ has provided an answer to this. In Christ our nature can be changed. We can be given a new birth and a new heart. We can be made new creations so that old things pass away and all becomes new. That is what the Gospel offers.

But if in unbelief we reject this provision of God's mercy then there is no other answer. There is no need to wait for the Day of Judgment to await God's verdict. The unbeliever is condemned already. What a fearful word is the word 'already'. It means a person can be sitting in church, singing hymns, taking communion and because he has never really believed in Christ he is already condemned by God.

In John 3 Nicodemus was clearly an unbeliever. He believed in God but he was an unbeliever. He believed all you needed in order to be acceptable to God was to be a Pharisee. The equivalent today is to believe all you need is to be a Catholic, or Methodist, or Anglican, or Baptist. He believed all you needed were the moral and religious duties of Phariseeism. As far as Jesus was concerned this meant Nicodemus was an unbeliever and condemned already by God.

What about *you?* In the New Testament meaning of the word, are *you* a believer or an unbeliever?

THE VERDICT

Having stressed the seriousness of unbelief in verse 18, Jesus goes on in verse 19 to declare God's verdict on man's refusal to believe the Gospel.

The word verdict immediately leads us to a picture of a courtroom. The Judge is there presiding over all the proceedings: the accused is in the dock: evidence is considered: witnesses are called and finally the verdict and the sentence are announced. This is a valid biblical picture. God is the Judge and we are the accused. The evidence in the context of John 3, is our attitude to Jesus Christ, that is our unbelief. It is not our behavior, not our morality, not our good deeds or our bad deeds, but our response to God sending His Son into the world to die on the cross for sinners.

All men are sinners by nature. According to Romans 5:12 we sinned in Adam, so we are born in sin and this brings upon us the divine judgment of death - "therefore, just as sin entered the world through one man, and death through sin, and in this way death came to all men, because all sinned." So before we even hear the Gospel sin has placed us under the sentence of death. This is all true, but in John 3 Jesus is dealing with the situation where sinners hear the Gospel and refuse to believe in the name of God's only begotten Son. This court scene is not some future Day of Judgment. It takes place *now*. It is true that there will be a Day of Judgment because the Bible says man is destined to die once, and after that to face judgment (Hebrews 9:27). But the verdict is now. Jesus says, the verdict has been pronounced and unbelievers are condemned already. When the Gospel comes to men it finds them already sinners under the wrath and judgment of God, but it presents to them an answer to that judgment. In the Gospel there is a full pardon offered to the vilest of sinners but that pardon depends upon a sinner believing in Jesus. Their unbelief brings upon them a new condemnation for which there is no remedy.

Light

Jesus now proceeds to show us the fairness of God's verdict. Men are born in sin, with a natural inclination to sin and it might be argued that if this is the case– can they be blamed? Yes, they can because God did not leave men in that condition. He sent light into the spiritual and moral darkness that is man's natural habitat. John Brown said, "Light is the symbol of knowledge as opposed to ignorance, of truth as opposed to error, of holiness as opposed to depravity." It is the same as saying that the means of obtaining knowledge and truth and holiness has been made available to men. Into this world so darkened by sin and into the minds of men so blinded by Satan, God in love and mercy and grace has sent light. And this light is Jesus.

He came to dispel the darkness. As the darkness of night retreats before the advancing light of the rising sun, so the darkness of sin cannot stand in the presence of the brilliant and dazzling holiness of Jesus, the Light of the world. So Jesus is able to break the power of sin in human hearts and reconcile guilty sinners to God. When God sent Jesus as Light into this world of sin it was the most wondrous thing he ever did. Even the sun shining in the heavens is but a dull glow compared to the light and beauty that radiates from Jesus.

To men and women caught in the all pervading darkness of their own sinful nature, God sends such Light as the world has never seen. So there is hope for sinners but men love darkness instead of light. Men prefer the things of depravity and spurn the light and beauty of Jesus. The reason for this rejection is not that the Gospel is too obscure to be understood, nor is it that the Gospel is too weakly supported with evidence to be believed. The reason, says Jesus, is because men's deeds are evil.

Evil

Evil is a very strong word, one we reserve for the vilest actions of men. Hitler was evil. Stalin was evil. Few if any would argue with that, but Jesus uses the same word to describe *all* unbelievers. Our pride might be offended by this but the word evil once again stresses how serious unbelief is. It is not just a matter of disagreeing with a doctrine or religious concept, it is a rejection of God and his gracious offer of salvation. While it may be obvious of some that their deeds are evil, where people simply have no love for Christ and the Gospel, Jesus says it is because their deeds are also evil. Their way of life may not be outrageous and they may be decent people by the accepted standards of society, but on the Day of Judgment, when the secrets of all hearts are made known, it will reveal them, by God's standards, to be evil. Men and women may reject the Gospel because they are openly immoral or criminals, or they may reject it because they are proud and selfish. Either way, says Jesus, it is because their deeds are evil.

Jesus does not stop there. In verse 20 he goes a step further and declares that such people hate the Light. That again is very obvious in some people. A Christian only has to speak to some friends or relatives about God to experience the strong and bitter reaction. The way that blasphemy has become an acceptable part of entertainment is evidence that people hate the Light. But Jesus is referring in verse 20 not to some unbelievers but to all unbelievers. There are many unconverted people who profess to like the Gospel. They enjoy singing hymns and may even enjoy hearing the Gospel preached, yet they remain unconverted. If a man does not hate the Light of God why does he not totally and unreservedly embrace it and come in repentance and faith to Jesus?

Jesus gives only one answer to that situation. It is for fear that his deeds will be exposed. If a man keeps away from the Light of God it is because his heart is all wrong. Have you ever picked up a large stone in the garden and seen the multitude of insects scampering away? They live in darkness and when light comes they flee from it. So too are unbelievers before the Gospel. Some flee and hurl abuse and condemn the Light. Others patronize it but keep it at arms length. Whatever reason men might give for remaining unbelievers they all stand under this verdict of God. Although man's salvation is entirely due to the grace of God, man's condemnation is his own fault. Light has come. Jesus has come. Atonement has been made for sin and guilt, and salvation is offered freely to all, but men love darkness instead of Light because their deeds are evil.

Good News

Darkness is the kingdom of Satan. It is bondage with an illusion of freedom, misery with a veneer of happiness, and it will end in hell. If men prefer this to God's light then the verdict cannot be argued with. There is no miscarriage of justice because this is the verdict of the Holy God, not of some fallible human judge. Consequently there is no appeal and the verdict stands.

The Verdict

In our courts there is only one thing that can change the verdict and that is if new evidence is produced that can show the verdict was wrongly arrived at. Is there any new evidence concerning us? It would not seem possible that there could be any because the Bible has clearly stated over and over again that we are all guilty. But the Gospel brings before God the Judge something new for him to consider. Jesus stands and pleads for us. He says, these guilty vile sinners have believed the Gospel and repented. They are Mine, He says. I love them. I died for them. I have clothed them with My own righteousness.

God the Judge responds to the plea of His Son. He must respond because it is God Himself who has instigated the Gospel. He says, they are now acceptable to Me but only because of Jesus. I pardoned them says the Judge. I justified them. And as a result, the verdict changes - they shall not perish but have eternal life.

This is the amazing message of the Gospel. We are guilty, of that there is no doubt, but Christ died for the ungodly and being justified by faith we have peace with God. For the guilty there is pardon and salvation but it is only as we believe in the Lord Jesus Christ.

NICODEMUS:
THE BORN AGAIN
CHRISTIAN

Verse 2 of John 3 tells us that Nicodemus came to see Jesus at night. The night visit was probably because he did not want to be seen. Nicodemus was a member of the Pharisee party, a group who were totally opposed to Jesus. At the point in time of John 3 Nicodemus was groping for the truth. We have already seen how difficult it was for him to unlearn all the religious views and interpretations of his upbringing, but still it is clear he did not share the outright rejection of Jesus that most of his fellow Pharisees so clearly manifested. In John 3 he is groping for truth but still very uncertain, so he is not too keen for his gropings to be made public. Perhaps his fellow Pharisees were right and Jesus was a fraud. He was not sure and he did not want to make a public fool of himself, so he talked to Jesus under the cover of darkness.

When we leave John 3 we have no knowledge as to how this man reacted to the very straight and direct talking of Jesus. The Savior did not mince words with this Pharisee. Nicodemus heard from the lips of Jesus that he needed to be born again. He was rebuked for his ignorance in spite of the fact that he was a teacher of Israel. He was told that those who do not believe in Jesus are condemned already by God, and that included him. How did Nicodemus react to this? What happened to him? Was he ever born again?

The next reference to Nicodemus is in John 7:50. This is a little over two years later and he is still groping for the truth. Two years after the John 3 interview with Jesus he is still not a believer, but there is a difference. Now he publicly defends Jesus before his fellow Pharisees. In verse 47 the Pharisees are furious with the temple guards for not arresting Jesus and they ask the sneering question of these underlings, whom they saw as being deceived by Jesus, "Has any of the rulers or of the Pharisees believed in him?" At that point one of their own number, Nicodemus, asks "Does our law condemn a man without first hearing him to find out what he is doing?" It is true that this was not much of a defense of Jesus. He was saying what any honest man ought to have said for any common criminal. But it was said, and said at a time when it was sure to arouse a bitter response as it did. Nicodemus is not yet a believer in Jesus but clearly there is something going on in his heart and he is not now like the rest of the Pharisees.

The next time we come across Nicodemus is in John 19:39. This is three years after John 3. Notice in this verse how John refers to Nicodemus as the man who earlier had visited Jesus by night. D. A. Carson[10] makes the point, "John may be telling us that by this action Nicodemus shows he is stepping out of the darkness and emerging into the light." I believe this is correct. Nicodemus is now making an open stance for Jesus. With Joseph of Aramathea he takes the body of Jesus from the cross and prepares it for burial. Joseph had been a secret disciple of Jesus. His fear of the Jews kept him from making an open profession of faith but now all that changes. Both Joseph and Nicodemus are changed by the death of Jesus and stand openly for him. John Calvin said, "Here we have striking proof that Christ's death was more quickening than his life. So great was the efficacy of that sweet savor which the death of Jesus conveyed to the minds of these two men, that it quickly extinguished all the passions of the flesh".[11]

Nicodemus was now a believer. He had been born again. It took three years after his initial meeting with Jesus, and perhaps by then the other Christians had written him off or forgotten about him. Perhaps he himself despaired of ever coming to true faith. Three years, but in the end the grace of God triumphed in this man. J. C. Ryle writes, "The case of Nicodemus is deeply instructive. It shows us how small and weak the beginning of true religion may be in the soul of a man. It shows us that we must not despair of any one because he begins with a little timid, secret inquiry after Christ. It shows us that there are wide differences and varieties in the characters of believers. Some are brought into full light at once, and take up the cross without delay. Others attain light very slowly, and halt long between two opinions. It shows us that those who make the least display at first, sometimes shine brightest and come out best at last. Nicodemus confessed his love to Christ when Peter, James, and Andrew, had all run away. What need we have for patience and charity in forming an estimate of other people's religion! There are more successors of Nicodemus in the church of Christ than we are aware of. We may see some marvelous changes in some persons, if we live with them a few years. The strongest, hardiest trees, are often the slowest in growth. He that sets down men and women as graceless and Godless, if they do not profess full assurance of hope the first day they take up religion and hear the Gospel, forgets the case of Nicodemus, and exhibits his own ignorance of the ways of the Spirit. All God's elect are led to Christ, undoubtedly, but not all at the same speed, or through the same experience."

Here is a great encouragement for Christians who have been witnessing to friends and praying for them for years. Often there appears to be little progress and we despair and are tempted to give up on them. This is also an encouragement for someone who may have been groping after salvation for years. Perhaps a few years ago Jesus seemed to speak so clearly to you, but nothing came of it. It may be that your attitude toward God is not as antagonistic as it was, and you may even defend the faith in arguments but you know that you are not born again. Nicodemus is a great encouragement to all in these situations. It took three years but the searching ended and faith was born in the seeker.

The salvation of a soul is the special work of the grace of God. It is a peculiar work, individually designed to each person, so that no two conversions are the same. True there are common ingredients like the need to hear the Gospel, conviction of sin and repentance (even this varies in degree from one person to another), but the circumstances will vary enormously. Some people are saved the first time they hear the Gospel, with others it takes years.

In the New Testament we see people coming to faith in Christ in many different ways. The background of the individuals varies, so too do the circumstances involved in their salvation. Consider how different the conversion experiences of Paul, the jailor at Philippi, Timothy and Lydia were.

Paul (Acts 9:1-22)
- from a deeply religious background
- dramatic and sudden
- saved on a particular date, at a particular place

Philippian Jailor (Acts 16:23-24)
- from a very worldly background, with no previous thought for God
- circumstances brought him to despair
- not seeking God, but found by him

Timothy (2 Timothy 3:15)
- brought up in a Christian home
- always known the scriptures
- cannot say exactly when he came to faith in Christ

Lydia (Acts 16:14-15)
- nothing dramatic
- seeking God for a long time
- the heart quietly opened to see and believe.

What we see in these four instances and in Nicodemus is that there is no outward pattern. There are no set of experiences common to all, but all are saved and born again

of the Holy Spirit. Circumstances and experiences may vary greatly but there are certain common factors. If you are a Christian it is because the Holy Spirit convicted you of sin and
- you realized your true condition (Luke 15:17-19)
- you repented (Acts 2:38)
- you believed (Acts 16:31)
- you received Christ (John 1:12).

If you are not a Christian it is because you have never been convicted of sin, never repented, never believed and received Christ as your Savior. Perhaps you are like Nicodemus in his first contact with Jesus and bewildered and confused by spiritual truths. It may be that your mind has never faced these things before. Do not give up now. Take heart from Nicodemus and seek the Lord earnestly. Jesus promised "Ask and it will be given to you; seek and you will find; knock and the door will be opened you. For everyone who asks receives; he who seeks finds; and to him who knocks the door will be opened" (Matthew 7:7-8).

End Notes

1 Expository Thoughts on John: Vol. 1, Banner of Truth, 1987. These volumes by Ryle on the Gospels are among the finest available in the world. Do yourself a favor and purchase them.

2 Note that the closing words of 2:25 seem to prepare the way for the opening words of chapter 3. "for He knew what was in man. There was a man." It appears that the Apostle John is using Nicodemus as one example of this group of men.

3 Redemption, Accomplished and Applied, pp. 79,80; Eerdmans Pub. Co., 1955.

4 Ibid., p. 103

5 Calvin's New Testament Commentaries, vol. 4, St. John, Part 1, Eerdmans Pub. Co., 1959

6 John Brown (1784-1858) Scotland's first professor of exegetical theology and one of Scotland's most influential ministers during the nineteenth century.

7 Charles H. Spurgeon (1834-1892) was an English Baptist preacher whose ministry touched and changed the lives of hundreds of thousands of people last century and whose writings are still used to minister over 100 years after his death.

8 See the book *Why I Will Never Become a Christian* by the same author which addresses this very issue.

9 Each of these three great Christian men are described in Peter Masters book Men of Purpose, published by The Wakeman Trust of London.

10 Don A. Carson is professor of New Testament at Trinity Evangelical Divinity School in Deerfield, Illinois. He is the author of several fine books, including a commentary on John's Gospel.

11 Calvin's NT Commentary, Vol. 5, p. 188.

Other Titles

published by

CALVARY PRESS

Stepping Heavenward -Elizabeth Prentiss

From Forgiven to Forgiving -Jay Adams

Thoughts for Young Men -J.C. Ryle

The Little Preacher -Elizabeth Prentiss

Heaven: A World of Love -Jonathan Edwards

A Dying Man's Regrets -Adolphe Monod

A Tearful Farewell from a Faithful Pastor -E. Griffin

You Know God's in Control -J.I. Packer

A Plea to Pray for Pastors -Gardiner Spring

Duties of Church Members -John Angell James

Marks of False Teachers -Thomas Brooks

Women Speaking in the Church -B.B. Warfield

To Order or inquire about this ministry;
call us toll-free at 1 800 789-8175 or
write us at: CALVARY BOX 805
P·R·E·S·S AMITYVILLE,
NEW YORK, 11701

Our Publishing Mission

CALVARY PRESS is firmly committed to print quality Christian literature which is relevant to the crying needs of the church and the world at the close of the 20th century. We unashamedly stand upon the foundation stones of the Reformation of the 16th century: Scripture alone, Faith alone, Grace alone and Christ alone! Our prayer for this new ministry is found in two portions taken from the Psalms: "And let the beauty of the LORD our God be upon us, And establish the work of our hands for us; Yes, establish the work of our hands." (Psalm 90:17) and "Not unto us, O LORD, not unto us, but to Your name give glory." (Psalm 115:1).